Volume 118 of the Yale Series of Younger Poets

Ward
Toward

Cindy Juyoung Ok

Foreword by Rae Armantrout

Yale
UNIVERSITY PRESS

New Haven and London

PUBLISHED WITH ASSISTANCE FROM
A GRANT TO HONOR JAMES MERRILL.

Yale University Press books may be purchased in
quantity for educational, business, or promotional use.
For information, please e-mail sales.press@yale.edu
(U.S. office) or sales@yaleup.co.uk (U.K. office).

Set in Yale New type by Motto Publishing Services.
Printed in the United States of America.

Library of Congress Control Number: 2023940081
ISBN 978-0-300-27391-5 (hardcover : alk. paper)
ISBN 978-0-300-27392-2 (paper : alk. paper)

A catalogue record for this book is available from the British Library.

This paper meets the requirements of
ANSI/NISO Z39.48-1992 (Permanence of Paper).

10 9 8 7 6 5 4 3 2 1

for my parents, and their parents, and theirs, and so on

Contents

III.

Foreword

This book is radically honest and unpretentious. Cindy Juyoung Ok never claims to know best. Her inquisitive, skeptical mind challenges beliefs, including any she herself might hold. The opening poem, "Three Act Comedy," begins "How dare you question my Eastern mystical status" and ends with "I don't believe in any thing, not even / the idea of California, no, I know, not even its sequoias." This is a book that questions personal identity while, at the same time, being deeply personal. Some of the poems are set in mental wards or describe an abusive relationship. Of a stay in the hospital, she writes, "I lobbied for the dignity to shit unsupervised." The way she frames this humiliating situation has a kind of self-deprecating humor. After all, we generally hear the words "I lobbied for" followed by the name of an industry or an NGO, not a bathroom privilege.

Ok's resistance to being categorized or labeled, evident throughout the book, may have begun in her experience as an Asian American or in her dealings with the medical establishment, but has become a poetics. Such resistance is evident in these lines, also from "Three Act Comedy": "Bone by bone, this poem erases adjectives—*green*, / *harsh, infinite*—and their stains. It becomes a student / of waiting when its coffin doesn't fit the hole, everybody / watching." This image is so ghoulish and so comic that it reminds me of Emily Dickinson. The poem/corpse is relieved of all its adjectival characteristics and it still won't fit in the (pigeon) hole. It was when I read these lines that I began to think this manuscript would be really good. It *is* true, by the way, that this book contains few adjectives. I'm pretty sure this is the first time in the history of literature that a poem has been described as a self-conscious corpse forced to endure a failed burial!

The poems in *Ward Toward* are full of dichotomies. For instance, in the poem "Moss and Marigold," Ok writes, "*my country* / provides an illusion of synthesis, as *my landlord* supplies // a fantasy of individuality." One can neither unite with others nor stand alone. This feeling of being in-between is familiar to many of us, I'm sure, but since Ok has family in both Korea and the United States, the feeling is charged. This is especially true when, in the United States, racist exclusion and even violence are added to the mix. Sometimes she expresses the distance she feels from her family traditions humorously, as in "Residue Guidelines," which begins "I was told not to shake / my foot that way— / the luck leaks out" and "Nights turn off your / fans, collect / your toenail // clippings." These are just two parts of a two-page deadpan list of such advice. (One senses the speaker is not apt to follow it.) At other times, she writes of this alienation with a sense of ambivalent guilt and regret. In "Mama I'm Sorry," she describes her books and degrees as betrayals.

Ok's poems depict other alienations she has felt. In the grimly hilarious poem "Laugh Track," she writes about two mental health clinics, one of which had only one nonwhite therapist. In the other, patients were given television sitcoms to watch while receiving magnetic brain stimulation (a treatment for depression). While undergoing the procedure, Ok discovers the racial politics of *Seinfeld*. In an astute analysis, she writes, "Barriers *Seinfeld*'s guest stars may face for us to laugh comfortably at include death, deportation, and disability, while the mess our four core characters build themselves is central, and free." For the poem's speaker, watching the sitcom causes pleasure—as she masters the plot devices—amid discomfort. When she is released from the clinic where she was shown *Seinfeld*, the doctor asks her to write a tribute to her treatment. It's gratifying to imagine the doctor reading this.

Hearing about the murder of Asian massage parlor workers in Atlanta is, of course, a more jarring experience. In the poem "In Atlanta," the speaker hears the words "massage" and "shooting" and instantly knows exactly what has happened, as if primed for this news. It is this instant knowledge that is part of the horror. Asian women have been forced into sex work or been subject to sexual violence in many countries that have experienced American wars and occupations. They become, as the poem puts it, a "beautiful // and disposable body . . . a metonym for wartime // sex, compulsive lure and, cheek to chink, / our famous flatness: breasts, feet, eyes, / consciousness." The poem aptly places the shooter as a soldier in a long war on Asian women.

Ok expresses the sense of division both formally and semantically. As if to embody the psychic fissures of contested spaces, several of Ok's poems, such as "Composition on a Raft," are divided in two facing columns. Cleaved spaces offer competing, and equally unsatisfactory, visions of home. She has learned to "question a dream from the inside," as she writes in "Clustering."

Along with the interweaving of her various themes, it's important to note that Cindy Juyoung Ok is a wonderfully inventive poet with a command of her craft. She writes in many forms, some invented, and her constant impulse is to break the frame, to escape oppressive containment. She will write a rhymed sonnet like "The Five Room Dance," using the final couplet to make what may be seen as a protest against imposed form:

> a closed round, the words we cross a swarm
> from which I am wrung. As I, wrong, form.

It is, of course, this sonnet that is "wrung"—a violent word—from the swarm of available words in a round. It is formed "wrong" because, though it has an ABAB rhyme scheme, it is not in iambic pentameter. There is another way we can read this, though. Who could "we" be here? All of us, I think. We are all born into the swarm, the "closed round" of our mother tongue. In the final line, Ok switches back to first person. It is *she* now who is wrung from language and forms "wrong." What I love most in these lines is the luscious play of sound, the unexpected rhyme of "swarm" and "form," the internal slant rhyme of "wrung" and "wrong," and the way the word "form" stands out at the end, almost wrong (because the word order is unconventional)—but beautiful.

She also writes poems that can *literally* be read in two ways. "The Orders" is a good example. It is written about a hospital stay, I'm guessing. It's written in quatrains, in which each line is numbered one through four. Each stanza can be read in the usual way, moving from one line down to the next. But they also make sense if you, for instance, read all the lines numbered 1 sequentially. For example, if we read the first three lines of the poem in the usual way, they read:

1. the only way out is all the way through
2. workbooks, each ending with a ☺ so big
3. it takes up a whole page of presentation

If you read the first three lines numbered 1, you get this:

1. the only way out is all the way through
2. quiet games they ask me to, changing
3. the rules, smiling to the hierarchy top:

Saying either that "the only way out" is through doing the workbooks *or* that the only way out is through playing "quiet games" makes perfect sense. The two statements contradict one another only because of the word "only."

I've seen poets try to use a form like this and fail; it can get awkward easily. For Ok, writing this poem could be one of the "quiet games" she plays to get out, to shake things up, to make sure we're paying attention. Reading her work is like being privy to several simultaneous trains of thought. Both the volta of her sonnet and the "games" she plays in "The Orders" can be seen as declarations of freedom. Ok will "form" as she chooses and is willing to take us along on a wild ride.

Rae Armantrout

I.

Three Act Comedy

I.

How dare you question my Eastern mystical status,
which I earned with bells the moon will never hear
and by enchantment with my body (its limits, mainly).
See: intensity as possessive. Theory as detachment.

What had happened was I happened not to die. Spit
out and over by a series of buildings, ward to ward,
adjustable beds and notarized briefs. See, I'm begging
you: apology as redundant. The microphone as penis.

II.

Bone by bone, this poem erases adjectives—*green,
harsh, infinite*—and their stains. It becomes a student
of waiting when its coffin doesn't fit the hole, everybody
watching. It had been a student of borders, of the spider

web on the cave marking time, of the age of trees in
colonized lands. And a child of resurrection, measuring
windows: the poem disrupts its own lure, doing
the work of the body: power modulated by convenience.

III.

I lobbied for the dignity to shit unsupervised, and
rain is romantic when you're rich and redeeming
your reputation as a domesticated wreck. Later I took
turns playing martyr with one who claimed to hate

birthdays rather than risk disappointment by another's
hand. What had happened was I left her. I think (See: plot
as Western) I don't believe in any thing, not even
the idea of California, no, I know, not even its sequoias.

Orientation

The stars are less bright
than the pictures, I report
to a friend who, after nine

years in prison, is still
shocked that when we were ten
I had not seen a cow.

When he asks me,
tenant of the language
in which I meet him, what

the outside is like, I offer
reluctant lines: the birds
sound more and more

like car alarms, and some have
begged for one that runs in
a minor key, but

quiet is so expensive
in this calendar, which runs
on a logic of *paradise*,

i.e., of grief. Attitudes
toward bells are proportional
to proximity, as public music

relies on the worship
of intimacy, and a belief
in the work: to foil

regret, to regard cement
as liquid, to fade eventually
well. In love, the teenagers'

eyes widen and their
grammar shrinks. Form outlives
us, but barely.

Laugh Track

I watched the half-hour 90s sitcom *Seinfeld* in chunks of 37 and a half minutes exactly: one full episode and a second minus its final act. Because the show follows a strict formula, this was not such a difficult loss. Each episode involves parallel storylines and in the last seven minutes, their plots collide; the two stories always wrap up synchronously, in farcical mischief.

I moved home after being hospitalized at my university's large hospital and enrolled in an outpatient program that at first required thirteen hours of individual and group therapy a week. I also went five mornings a week to the edge of a valley for magnetic brain therapy, then off-label, by which a coil on my head created short and regular pulses. The nurse who put on *Seinfeld* and monitored the machine once said she only slept four hours a night. She followed up with "bodies are built differently," but privately I wondered.

The gap between farce and comedy is that there are no stakes in farce. Barriers *Seinfeld*'s guest stars may face for us to laugh comfortably at include death, deportation, and disability, while the mess our four core characters build themselves is central and free. In this way, it mirrors melodrama.

At the outpatient center, there was one nonwhite therapist on staff. In a morning group in my last month, he stated plainly that initially, I had participated generously through others' stories, making logical connections, but fiercely avoided sharing personal information or emotional capacity. Lately this had changed, he said, as had my body language. I was on the couch, suddenly aware of my positioning in the room, wearing a long skirt I had on when, at student health the semester before, a nurse asked me when I was due. I had gained weight on my medication that held strangely abdominally on a slight frame, not so much unrecognizable as imbalanced.

The first episode of each session primed me to the show format, and in the second episode, I guessed the upcoming climax, which seemed somehow received, inevitable. If two characters are involved in one plot and two in another (or three and one; two, one, and one), those in the major plot cross over with the others, everyone surprised or confused, a misunderstanding cited and some wordplay included. Counting down in units of 37 and a half minutes, prediction always came, the ending's physical comedy presumed.

As I finished the magnetic therapy and in the middle of the outpatient talk sessions, I started walking around my quiet neighborhood once a week. I no longer needed my strategy for crawling gradually out of bed, by which I slapped one arm across my torso and concentrated on pointing my weight toward its end and onto the ground. In some ways the procedure had become easier since I had gone off medication and was thin again, but in this step, the lack of mass limited my body. I hadn't known when people said they could not get out of bed, it was so literal. As a child, I potty trained easily and early, but at nineteen, I wet my bed twice because I couldn't get out of it.

There were two options for shows at the small private office, and *Seinfeld* was the highbrow one. It was the tapering last days of DVD reign, and whichever disc had been on from the previous day's last patient was the one I stayed on come morning. Over time, there was a sense that these characters lived in a timeless space across season, perpetually amid shenanigans, skillfully keeping interactions with nonwhite guest actors under 90 seconds.

The therapist and I were surrounded by white women during the morning session proclaiming my past self an unwilling team member. He reported that our shared country of heritage had one of the highest suicide rates in the world, with almost no therapy, and a study in the news had recently marked its rates highest (its women, especially). I don't know how he knew invoking this superlative would comfort me rather than make me feel doomed.

In the magnetic therapy waiting room, I often read the testimonials in their plastic sheet protectors. Some said they had tried everything, including ECT (electroshock, I had learned in group, was an outdated term), but only the magnets worked, worked like nothing else. They had struggled, they wrote, to keep a job, maintain relationships, expect food and shelter; here they had written pull quotes, and only the well perform favors so intimate. These were grownups, I thought, people in their 40s, 60s. I pitied them, how long they had waited to be charmed by Elaine on their screens, to be concerned about the sleepless, mistaken nurse. I was still a teenager, I noted to myself. I could still become a doctor, a teacher, or a painter with little humiliation.

I felt relief about the statistic that seemed to explain my lack of inciting factors. It was obviously ancestral, I thought, from all the occupations. And at my age, my parents would have been able to explain their suffering. Protesting a military dictator, they were grateful to not be kept longer in prison or hit harder with a baton. My choice to leave a college styled like a resort seemed stranger. I was comforted, too, reading that the length of a first episode of major depressive disorder is frequently nine to twelve months (mine, eleven). I turned the page to another figure: 80% of people who have their first episode before the age of twenty have another in their lifetime. I had a short urge to refute this second source. How was an episode measured? Was it peer-reviewed and replicated? I wanted, again, to be an exception.

Around the period when I started walking, I began writing about what was happening in the past tense, hoping to create some distance between the events—the calls, the ambulance, the appointments—and my day. The outpatient doctors said I had been receptive of, and benefited from, talk therapy. The magnet doctor asked me to write a testimonial for her website.

I thought for many months it was the secret wish of all my loved ones that I would die, forgiving their burden. On an apartment rooftop the next summer I admitted this to two friends, who responded with shock. One said it would have been the worst thing to happen to them. I learned later that in the East this is a more reasonable delusion: suicide as service—as offering.

What made *Seinfeld* good was that our protagonists were bad (selfish, disloyal, impulsive) and didn't claim much else. Only in adding obstacle or creating a mood of disorder could their stories close. In farce, there is no cliffhanger, only images of cliffs, glorious in their familiar awkwardness. Each episode ends on a new problem, but the resolution, which might be boring, is off screen, never to be mentioned in the episodes that follow.

"P.S. Please Forgive Poor Grammar"

Maybe you are not
wake up yet. Today is another
new day God allows us. I can't
say I understand
your feeling totally.
But I remembered
being your age.

At that time I need
to decide I live
normal life or commit
for movement. When I thought
about parents, I couldn't decide
easily. I almost think
about death instead of getting
through. Even I was nineteen
I felt like I had lived whole
my life. Two of my friends
burnt their body to protest.
Every day I feel shade
of death near me.
I overcame the material
value like money or
name at that time.

Now I felt that
agony made me more
spiritual rather worldy. I
appreciated my struggling
time after twenty-five years.
But still somebody ask me
start my twenties again,
I will say no.

Eight years ago
I went to see two boys
grave. I felt so sorry about them.
If they live now, they can see
how our country is
better now.

Moss and Marigold

My country is broken, is estranged, is trying, we write,
as though there is such a material as a country, as
though the landlord doesn't charge rent for life lived
outside the house. When it comes to survival there is no right

way but there's no wrong way either. The country is
a construction, with each writing becomes more made.
I am making it now, here, to you—to say *my country*
provides an illusion of synthesis, as *my landlord* supplies

a fantasy of individuality. When I picture a country,
the ground is newly stormed—the snow a kind of revision
in its refusal of fission. But when I imagine the suburbs,
it is always sunny, with caution tape around oak trees,

landline lights blinking, and pictures of parents laid
as bookmark: janitors mopping against time, office workers
counting. The city's in my name and its only borders
are my body's, my counted and settled and made state.

Before the DMZ

My
moth-
er sent
a photo of
the federal build-
ing she was
being naturalized in,
writing, Boring I
love   you. That winter
her father   revealed he left
behind a first wife, two kids, north
before the war, the news unremarkable
because *For us, everybody had somebody they—*
So my mother hired an investigator; visited
because, newly American, she could. She flew
south after, and on her photos, he pointed at
the 67-year-old he had last known at seven.
Said, *She was smart. She was really smart.*
Within a year he lost his memory to
stroke. He cried when they
tied him so he could not
pull his tubes out and
my mother had only seen
him cry when the special ran
on public broadcast. Ten thou-
sand families reunited while every-
one watched. Doesn't anyone k-
now this person? Live calls, arti-   Gen-
facts, tears—she watched   erally no
him watch.   one recalled where
they had been separated.
But a ripped hem, or rules
of a childhood game, that big
mole. A port of waiting. I al-
ways wanted to hate binary
but I grew up here where the
cure to forgetting a stubborn
chorus is doing simple arithmetic. Her
trip north was strange, formal—
delicate words, doubtful gestures.
She noticed the brother had pso-
riasis on his knuckles and hid her
laughter in a corner, her scars proof
of genes that had skipped the one
brother she knew. The countries
are linked by land—mostly, I know,
by an area covered in stone. I ima-
gine jade-colored water between
them, a wide, boring o-
cean on the thirty-
eighth
parallel.

Fissured

Several of my bones have splintered or
separated and been left to heal incorrectly
on their own, mostly in childhood. Of course
the analyst believes this to be symbolic
of my habitual denial of pain or, indeed,
vulnerability, but she cannot admit this directly.
She asks me leading questions like, am I truly
feeling the feeling of suffering, which I
find difficult to imagine. If I'm not feeling
my pain, then who or what is the me in *my*?
Instead, I announce that my partner notes
often how I never complain, rarely experience
side effects of medications or symptoms
of an illness. By providing evidence for her
claim, I try leading her to incidentally provide
some reasoning. I know she thinks this hope
for narrative arrangement, too, reflects repression
of some deep ache. Still, I conceive of physical pain
as an intellectual relief, whereby thought stops
being the primary expression. I read that Asian
patients require less analgesic than the European
ones and wonder about what I want, my Asian
patience, against what I require. My twice broken
nose creates a sort of suffocating zig zag,
permanent purple band along my bridge, so
light it is imperceptible to almost everyone.
An elbow to my face in front of a group made
them suddenly concerned, so I smiled to render
such disquiet unnecessary. I could not assume
their concern was real, which is to say lasting,
and I held, as I hold now, pain as ultimately
shallow, never indicative of anything but itself.

The Orders

1. the only way out is all the way through
2. workbooks, each ending with a ☺ so big
3. it takes up a whole page of presentation
4. on acceptability of the standard: I play

1. quiet games they ask me to, changing
2. and wide, accept diagnoses, and I write
3. in my narrow notebook to list visitors,
4. conversations, books, hoping to escape

1. the rules, smiling to the hierarchy top:
2. my pride as the social worker's favorite,
3. friends who prove I can exist beyond
4. conditions of involuntary commitment,

1. my courtyard privilege (CYP), a daily
2. walk to an enclosed outdoors, heaven
3. though some do seem frightened of
4. leaving our LV ward, one nurse always

1. reminding that we do not have *rights*
2. of grass, one tree, brick walls, scratched
3. me: signs of suicidal ideation, a loss of
4. jokes as an acronym for Looney Ville,

1. but *privilege*, to feel rain on our skin or
2. messages in rocks, trite or radical,
3. bathroom solitude—these try to make
4. a home, offer a dignified time designated

1. to eat a second sandwich, discuss how
2. almost dying is boring, mostly, and all
3. gossip, creating a true market by which
4. as a person with psychiatric disabilities

1.   the therapist looking just like Sally Field
2.   is delusion, a way to make familiar my
3.   washed hair and completed workbooks
4.   by the state and allow the fluorescence

1.   from our movie memories, may accuse
2.   unfamiliar part-time caretakers who
3.   can buy me freedoms and personhoods
4.   of cafeterias and neon white bedrooms

1.   we make up; quarantined from music, I
2.   call most perception hallucination since
3.   I will not know until the discharge of
4.   my body thinned at its own perimeters,

1.   brought through our dessembly line,
2.   sets of morning measurements, pills,
3.   questions about my mind's intention
4.   which, like ward windows, held gaps.

Pale Music

I was in love, once, and when the mothering was over
we didn't know where to look or how to hang our hands.

They say the mountains in Utah look just like the ones in
Afghanistan, except at a certain set of angles to be avoided.

Altar boys often get dizzy on the job. Some blame
the candles, but sushi chefs know not to lock their knees.

There is a caterpillar born to explode, releasing virus
from the tops of trees to spread it through their skin bits.

Everything looks fragile in profile, and do you ever sit
on the toilet wishing Jerusalem meant something to you?

Beings from another orbit would think we hate the rain,
revolving ourselves around its prospect or memory.

We tend to the myths we deserve, like the integrity of
the necklace, or that good tissue is not sacrificed in vain.

It is the study of the foreign object versus self-object,
solving those instances where a body cannot recognize

something as itself. Unlike butterflies, who cannot fly
without sun, caterpillars fear the light, train not to climb.

Terms and Conditions

You call me ho; it's short for home.
A cockroach falls from a chandelier
and my bodega loyalty fluctuates in
pace with the funeral's bloody nose.
I've been eating trees my whole life,
which usually made me more patient
but more cruel; recently I stood on
a porch that wraps around that nest,
the house that used me. Any noise
can be a curse to a child of chaos,
silent hallways from Gothic novels
to twilight wind in fire songs. This
unlucky, to not even be an architect
and to be inundated with the prose
of it all—were we, daughters, spent,
while all hoped for sums? You call
out ha; it's short for harvest. To be
a child is to gather secrets, an elder
to risk in transit. Once when I was
recovering, covering again myself,
I confused sharing for stealing, read
murder into shadows until laughter
came from silhouettes. I've since
fazed, piano bleaching the scene,
becoming the fog and the pulp. You
name me ma; I know it means mine.

The Tyranny of Representation

Even if you counted every song
in which the word California appears
and even if you return yourself to your

first form. Even if you are the friend
of your instrument and the marsh of
your family, even if you have

sliced brains into one hundred
twenty disks a piece to place them
on clear rectangular slides, even if

everyone is reasonable after your
mom has just died. Even if you have
twirled at every rest stop, paid

the price of the present, recognized
shame as generic—still no event is
like blindness, no idea is like

prison, even if you promise you
describe last night's little dream, even
if you study and consider the conditions

of planthood and metaphor, know
dying is not like death and not even life
is lifelike. There are photographs

of small children laughing in black
and white that people stop and cry at
in museums but ignore in homes.

I Was a Highly Awarded

child, worked hard to be
beloved by whichever
adults were accessible.
Pretending I sought to
be average in hopes of
social acceptance was
a part of the technique,
because I knew I could
always establish status
and belonging through
concerted effort around
generosity. I assumed
reading first, listening
fast, and remembering
the details of your most
boring story about that
second cousin was my
path to earned intimacy,
to joy. When I became
a ward of the state, all
rights paused, and while,
against my will, a non-
individual, I found that
precocious pays no bills
and the production of
devotion offers little in
the way of tenderness.

Clustering

This is not a planetarium. Not even
a dissolution of expiration dates. My people
eat both small and large intestines, and
I respect anybody in touch with their rage.

I question a dream from the inside and
everything I do is to be remembered.
Anyway, only language can interrupt
conviction, divorce from the tide.

It's been a long time now but it's easy
to list the things I am not: my name,
the hair on my arm, difficult to delight.
We call autumn here very early spring and

wishing is about release in every heat:
petal off, lantern up, lash away, salt over.
Cities keep running out of grave space,
and teachers have to guard like athletes.

And since no one is listening, I might
as well say that peeing in my sleep—
it was a way of preserving integrity. Of
knowing it is my femurs I can recognize.

Park Street

Everyone is envious of those more
alive than them and when we are not
aware of this we are directed by spite.

I once felt a long absence of the magic
and the summer after the sense passed,
I visited the city where I had been

young, walking street corners on which I
had cried out of an absorption with an idea
of myself and with a desire to be

witnessed, to be made public. Curtains were
drawn on the room where I had been changing
when I noticed a man walking repeatedly past,

presumably to watch the silhouette of
the nude figure through a crack in the linen.
Longing is always a threat but

that which is longed after is not the threat
nor is it the threatened. The town had
spread and melted, promising again that

with time, the concept of a heart—
of any central location—diminishes.

Composition of a Raft

Ramallah, Palestine

Elsewhere they carried out
in the earth to pause the wildfires—
stretching time, wandering past
the myths we kept like keys
born of attachment

planned explosions of clay
that summer we were
the blockades, telling
and studying loyalty
not alignment

They counted hundreds of
sea turtles, touching like
we were caging and
comparisons tend to stifle
so we leaned not leaped—
to want anything that much

washed up dead
lovers that summer—
sifting because
both things
we didn't want

It was the longest loss
for a century that summer—
putting everyone back
and avoiding spectacle,
spectator, resisting
in pieces

of the moonview
we spent the dream
in their places
by refusing to play
the humiliation

That summer we learned
that exile is always story—
remembering to call back or
supply, despite our knowing
like panic

to bargain with gods,
we were never
predicting the water
—how much relief is
in promise

Surviving Inklings

You lose friends to both
death and unusually lively
withdrawal, as well as give

some up, as anticipated,
to misunderstanding. You
leave those you assured

you would not leave and,
too, people have left
you in silence and without

reason but presumably
because of your intensity,
which you have long heard

from friends, never lovers,
for whom it was the draw.
When you leave you rarely

think about those left, so
perhaps such it is for
those who leave you:

typically no story, with
every tensile explanation
partial, each narrative

convenient, and changing.
You reserve the secrets
of theirs you remember,

pray occasionally for their
families, and praise silently
some whistle of generosity

you witnessed. You forget
the contours slowly in
the long second leaving,

neutrality a structure
you learned to glamorize,
the way you have come to

imagine doors as rectangular.
Under limits of the boxy
entry, you think of cities

as grids, describe a bird as
the tint of ink, forgetting
that ink can be any color.

II.

Tally of What Names

Better than safety
is the idea of safety,
the long noodles'
solid egg grazing
liquid yolk. I am
not in a field: what maims
the house maims me.

This is the least far we
have been, so far
from far, not a crown
nor memory of the circus,
its crowd. Sitting broad,
rationing dresses, I see
rumors now steep against
the board like the balmed
violence of summer. I
am not a field: you
carve and I'm untended,
hospitable to the minor
chords I crave, and you say
the yoke's unintended.

Ward of One

Confined by a lease with a beloved man
who declared again and again that he waved
the kitchen knife toward me not to gash

but to indicate, only point, my body became
a district of our home, calculating his
gestures and wondering if the signs

would match their means. One night I said
the character's joke in a movie reminded
me of him and at his reaction ran away—

I tried, please imagine—but he blocked
the door and held my key, planned
aloud to drive the river into my car, but

he meant my car into the river, so perhaps
he truly believed he had pointed the blade
tip to himself and not to my crouching

chest. True, he punched the square of bed
next to my face and not my face, slapped
the wall just above my head to inform

me. Such symbols could be figures: I
sat in a quiet room when he entered to
yell that he would sue me for twelve

thousand dollars and I stayed so still as he
described my domestic sins: various names
for my allotted gender. There was a spot

on the floor where I would lie as I waited
for his rage to pass into grief, and there
I would remember that I was once

the youngest child with glasses
in the history of my optometrist's office
and that after they broke in class I taped

the bridge and my teacher smiled. Or
I'd picture these small pastel drawings
I made then—long-eared dogs,

cobalt skies, a striped beach ball, drawn
from memory, taped on the walls I shared
with my sister, proud of how I saw.

When he wished me dead I whispered to
myself the word lucky, reminded myself
I was, because my parents at least

wanted me to live—there were people
who did not wish me dead. Later he explained
his fists had been for emphasis and would

never have been laid; he laughed, saying
the number twelve thousand, my ransom,
was random, and he was sorry—impossible

—though I felt so sorry when in that year,
in that house, I found my circumstances
betraying the love I had tried to inherit.

The Five Room Dance

In a search for more proportionate address we leak
out of bed as you stretch your books and I mine
the frozen language for olding hands day by week.
I account for each siren and you count the hips to sigh

over with the seam of open borders. Tracing the yard,
the lace of leaves as why I write. Why I, right, frown
your side affects, the cadence of the fact that stars:
a woman is a thing that absorbs. Reset by our brown

paper walls, time lends rest (flooding fast the thread
where we once swam to worship, prepared mourning
feasts, and, at last, lashed all the ideas we wed).
I'm sorry we need to be bodies here, five doors in

a closed round, the words we cross a swarm
from which I am wrung. As I, wrong, form.

Shakeout

As a child, I went to extremes.
Are you listening, are you listing?

The constructions we know of
holiness and madness converged

only later. Ambulances are cradled
and dolls go to war for the same

reason the word elegy appears
so often in poems. There are places

where shaking is expected, loss is
assumed. You and everyone should

applaud my labored nonchalance!
Luckily I happen to know that

coyotes love cemeteries and vertigo
onset is typical in such a clean gallery.

This is the part of every night
you honor the years you had person

permanence. But of course stillwater is
only still internally, and still moves

when a tire is passed across it and back
as pagodas assimilate like peninsulas,

who have all gone agnostic, switching
prison cells. When did the world turn

color? As a child, you went to extremes.
With the proudest discretion I bleed

what I idolize, I cannot know. And
then meet the wonder in each irritation.

Nap Plot

The mass stabbing had long impended—we
knew before they told us. Maybe something
about body language. Their plans were taut,

clean. We knew well we would be dead soon.
Being contained was one thing, but the end
of the breath would be notable, new. All this

in the woods, cages enforced invisibly. Holding
my hair up, I thought, *if everything is inevitable,
then nothing is*. If I had this power to deny these

facts of death, I had the power of god. I knew
I would beg. I was a beggar. The man in charge,
full of charm and rage, was adored by helpers,

mostly women. In the dream, they were homely
and I wasn't. Well, I wanted to live. Waiting,
we looked down at our fingernails and shuffled

in small concentric circles. I went to meet with
him in a little office with some of us huddled
on one side. Them and their knives on the other.

I was there to prevent unnecessary dying in
general. But also, I told you, I wanted to live.
In this hope, supposed myself an individual.

The others a mass. Even my family—they were
a part of the everyone I wanted to save, my sister
appearing as a baby. As I had heard always in

my mother's voice: *They would throw our babies up and catch them on their swords, you know.* Likely a sort of elaboration. Still, I had to make the man laugh.

I was to acknowledge his sense of self. It was
helpful to list features that sounded specific
but could apply widely. The game was not sexual,

or complicated. I held social sway and I hated
it, all that was fixed. In the end he gave me
evacuation in addition to survival. And he asked

nothing. I saw he was suffering and I hoped
he would not, though this was outside my locus
of concern. I left, took a nap, still in the woods.

Others filed back into the cities. When I woke,
the grounds were a vacation space, adorned. Elderly
couples played cards on wooden benches.

The tide was low beneath a deck painted green.
It was maybe an island now, in a bay. I walked
barefoot on a dirt path, where some from my original

group circled around a red grocery cart. They
stared at the pile in it, at work on a new question.
What do you do with the blades once the mass

stabber has been appeased? We considered ocean,
towels. Taped boxes with handwritten warnings
not to open. There was this idea that sharpness

could not be unloaded. That in this last step,
we might easily multiply harm. Briefly, we
contemplated burial. The conversation was not

audible or visual, but transmitted among
the various variants of myself, like in all my
dreams. A negotiation of logic, finally, a proof.

Patch

I know how the bats get
in the house and I know

catharsis is not the ideal.
Before this I only knew

the city, so poor in iron
and trains but was called

flat-faced by a stranger
and I was planting yes

I was panting. I wanted
to be the close of desire,

to be an object of some
verb. Heard the instant

of a punch's bloom and
found it soundless, then

refused to learn dances
with names. The canal

I walked past mornings
on an all-ledge bridge

(must have in evenings,
then, too) held the milky

swans who seemed to be
sleeping as they tended

to the soft bellies of their
wings. Swanhood is not

greedy, once apart from
the herd they do grieve.

Bats can yell, too, eyes
narrowing, yellowing—

it ends when they can
explain the beginning.

Leave Her to Heaven

It was, for us, a city of proxies. You counted
your prospective ailments, awaiting your health
by planning its loss. Elsewhere, cicadas were back

and secret parties were cast, but we watched the thick
river pass around us, synecdoche for its human
pollutants, and we tended the swell of gray weeds

that was nevertheless a garden. All that spring
any object could be a door and the brick red of eggs
in purgatorio, suspended in the pan, overlapping

like neighbors, indicated what we knew but wanted
constantly confirmed—that withstanding is just
waiting. With a temporary patience I held

grudges like babies as I bled generously across
weeks, tinting my legs with layers of the remnants
of curdled brown clots I would finger. Every place

we moved to after represents and abandons
the first, reminding us you can learn from what
you do not treasure. It was where we covered

even the windows in grocery bags, knifed a couch
on one side to extract stray objects, danced lying
down in late morning light, hoping for a day of

mildness. You had conjured your deprivation in
detail to prevent it but affliction chose me, spotlight
sprained into sky light. I felt grateful then to smell

a trace of dull copper as fluid evaporated, asked you
to account for my body's inventory by weighing
and describing the blotted towels, a brisk order

by which we agreed to an exchange: for me
to imagine pain, for you to experience it. In
the dream I explain one dawn, there is no means

out of the strawberry gang. Mashed and rotting
cartons of dark pink clumps cover my childhood
kitchen where our bid to leave the scheme is denied.

Ten Sessions

1: Client reported that she is
      severe   help

2:                       to
      a   violence hotline   ashamed
   in   position

                           on eggshells.
    a
          remorse

for   health

           strongly discouraged

                       about
     being violently
receptive   . She agreed   911 should

3:           stay   in bed

with   safety plan

          not willing to   police
  nor   willing to   friend.
       access

          is trying   .

4:
           names

            called   hotlines
                 with

reluctance to leave

5:   this week.

6:

                         tend   calm
        to enrage   further
             to engage   .

7:                          She

        keeps

                     for   it is time to
leave.

8: Client

                make sense

         .

9:
       she confronts   vows

                          in   effort   patterns

10:                  distressed by   decision

and embarrassed

                                      to remember

       .

Ten Sessions

Client reported that she is severe
help to a violence
hotline, ashamed in position
on eggshells. A remorse for health
strongly discouraged about being
violently receptive. She agreed
911 should stay in bed—
with safety plan, not willing
to police nor willing to friend.
Access is trying. Names called hotlines
with reluctance to leave this
week. Tend calm to enrage further,
to engage: she keeps for it is time
to leave. Client, make sense.
She confronts vows in effort
patterns, distressed by decision
and embarrassed to remember.

It Is Like

the baby's shock at first light, weeping.

The metaphors for panic dissatisfy me
by comparing the internal to the external
—weight, containment, suffocation,
screaming, itching—which it is not like.
I have known well molasses and bubbles
and I'm sorry but it is not a plural substance
nor is it a place, not an enclosed elevator or
some classy cliff. It is the moment of
the first, a moment that becomes a life.
It is like melting; it is like wanting and
even so it is like not wanting. It refuses,
I promise, all language, and requires
the ruination of the self, of narration.

The opposite of resignation, the startle
extends, leaving relief only in accepting
the diminishing options: sink water is cool
to the dunk, and a hum can slow the heart's
beat. Physical exertion also confuses
memory into thinking there is no terror,
only strain. The baby, too, is tricked
eventually into betrayal—stroking light
switches, beginning to speak. But when
it is like what it is like, these materials
are too effortful and the quickening
song of the ringing phone does not console
when the body comes to be its panic.

Ten Words

I was not able to hear whispers well as a child and I worried this would cut short my friendships.

At that school a teacher let us do creative assignments about the origin of our ten weekly vocabulary words.

It seemed important not to ask another child more than once or twice to repeat their secrets.

I wrote about the word "dire" as coming from a town that punished residents with an offering: *die or consequence?*

Many ESL programs use cognates as a bridge, a strategy mostly relevant from European languages.

Everyone picked consequence and eventually the question became *dire consequence?*

Children of parents born elsewhere sometimes overcorrect for their parents' pronunciations.

The consequence was comparable to death so it could be assumed to be always dire.

A Spanish-speaking child might mentally remove their parents' *e* sounds before *s* at the beginning of a word.

My mother's wedding dress was rented and her mother made Christmas trees of umbrellas.

Or a Korean-speaking child might mentally trade their parents' *l*'s and *r*'s in the middle of a word.

Another fable I wrote, for the word lackadaisical, had to do with some lack of daisies.

The two children would then alternatively overcorrect the English "establish" to *stablish* and *estabrish*.

I first learned the language at a pre-school whose blue nap cots and wide slide I remember.

Hypercorrection reveals an anxiety around the appearance of knowing and belonging.

To tell that story, I first had to tell the schema of daisies and what they had represented.

There are distinctions which are difficult to learn about a language from textbooks, manuals, and calendars.

I was competent, teachers assured my parents, just silent as I socialized with the other toddlers.

For example, it is not obvious "I lie like a semi-colon across the white bed" presents two meanings.

When I wore my shoes on the wrong feet for my knock knees, classmates followed in reciprocal silence.

Reading with language only as vehicle will rarely indicate that "lay" provides two tenses.

When I started talking, after several months of teachers' concern, they say I spoke paragraphs.

In Atlanta

I danced with the niece of a friend
some springs back, a trip on which
their matriarch called me family.

That winter, the city was a shock
of snow and she wrote asking for tips
on uncovering her paled car. She had

told us already of the white hoods
who march, how she had watched
outside church at seven in black pigtails.

Last week I heard *shooting* and *massage*;
in the instant of hearing knew, then said,
all that had not yet been reported. From

form to form I always was a good tester:
fill in the blank, circle the best—
When the checkboxed of our kind

is mowed, there is not a fear of new
attention but of what is revealed as abiding,
realities confirmed about my beautiful

and disposable body, effortlessly endable,
after all a symbol, even in hiding,
and my title a metonym for wartime

sex, compulsive lure and, cheek to chink,
our famous flatness: breasts, feet, eyes,
consciousness. Every mother knows

that any child's long life is a sustained
surrender—the math of one man's really
bad day, our millions of hearts buried.

Bartender's Bargain

Listen I'm young and I know something
about plum noodles and de-escalation as

the only tender who doesn't drink. Oh, and
the translation of lunar measures of time.

When bitten, ignore the instinct to pull, instead
pushing the latched body part further into

the biting mouth. This will lead to release,
though perhaps then it all starts again. How

many of us can say we have saved anything,
let alone money. We'll discuss the impulse

to claim the dead, but please acknowledge
first the randomness of maps, and, sure,

of attachment. Wash and either pickle,
grill, or boil fruits (organize your decision

as usual—around avoiding nausea). We work
here but we don't decide the prices and

still we take responsibility, we do, for this, and
for wind, and, yes, certainly, for our patterns.

Rights

No skin cream is innocent, not corduroys, no flushable wipes. All objects are made and named and positioned, the same way the writers of crossword puzzles make implicit and treacherous assumptions around knowledge.

Warding off illness, I continue to live, not knowing how to pronounce cicada, being both settler and character. There are fewer people here I can be mistaken for than anywhere I have lived, a proud and frivolous itemization.

Given the power to write the clues for others to cross, mine would be dramatically unrelated to any czar or tzar, like nine or ten letters uttered to deny the evil eye or six-letter mononym of she who does not know her.

The left lung is smaller than the right. Oboists practice a circular breath, stored covertly in cheeks, but fans who watch their mouths too closely sometimes faint, not breathing at all instead of invisibly like the performers.

Two friends once gave me lice without our realizing and, after their de-licing visit, I passed it back and we all had to return to the same salon. Symbols, too, have this contagion—sharing and mediating blame and punishment.

As pressure inside reconciles to match the atmosphere, shoulder blades protect the lungs, which are longer than most generally picture, and which stay massaged from the inside by two kidneys, one wider by a centimeter.

Far from family now, I am confused not for individuals but for other groups. I become an index for the unknown, for the invasive, or maybe I am an icon, and also a tribute, like an old etching on the underside of a school desk.

The mobility of the wrapping ribs guides air, whether the breathing is voluntary, which is typical, or involuntary, in crisis. Accessory muscles like abdominals are at work; these participate but they never themselves initiate.

It is cold to be thin, to know borders between bodies this constantly. Words can, too, be body, the O of hands and mouths and volume's aspiration: oboe, O, old, O, own. O, I wake up now and here O. Or I O, O. No I. O. O

Table of Contexts

I stay outstretched in a November
coat, not abundant and not wanting
to be. Having been spit on, sat on,

I hope not to mind, or mine, being
pathetic, but keep loving to be pitied
for trivial troubles. A machine I own

mistook *shootings* for *students* in a transcript,
ushering me to tilt canals toward titles
and curate hedges into pages. I had

thought I was a shape but it is a form
of furniture, not a prop but not yet
a structure, the way I eat with pairs

of sticks and repeat the attic antics
outside my house. There is always
wartime here so I do render to reenter,

stir to thirst, offer this crate of skin,
roster of resting text (you can eat
the paper). Not a performer, I know

the figure of the student exceeds—
includes—that of the teacher and I think
it is for you I wash and rotate the wish.

Curtain

When I say we wait on the dead I
mean star maps are sold on every corner,

because to mention color is to speak
on language. Is abstraction still luxury

in a world in which—suppose—you don't
feel watched? In the way that moral preferences are

aesthetic judgments, or how simile has gone out
of style. Is there an art that does not serve

the interests of the notebooks in
power? I have enough

cousins and if you've been
to an annual party for a ghost you know

most architecture is about spilling.
So only the rich leave bones

on rice like each grain isn't fragile,
and people pray to be close

to the ground, spelling, as in the study
of lightning, ground and space based

measurements. The house can also betray
by not existing: where there is no

original loss, one or several are
fashioned. Instead of romanticizing

subtlety, I dream in English with
the confidence of a private pool.

III.

The End of Crisis

When you leap over the deer carcasses
that line every garden you will marvel
at their tidiness, at how bloodless a death
by drought can be. When I crawl through
the highway pieces shattered by heat,
I will admire the clean slits as I kick
aside crumbles of broken stone with little
blistering. When you thread between
the overtaken shores and bodies of elders,
frozen, when I follow the fallen saplings'
directions toward the horizon where
colorless sky and earth meet, we will
remember rippling at the birthday parties
for corporations and framing the ash
of beloved photos burnt in wildfire. When
we think of crossing the river to each
other, you from the gorge of the landslide
to me at the crest of the typhoon, it is then
we will find ourselves in a dead imaginary,
in some fictive past where the *you* exists,
where *I* is not a myth we use to keep
surviving at the cost of bird and glacier,
home and tenderness. Once we have ruined
the future of becoming fossils, we will
know finally we die not for drowned sea
turtles or swarming locusts, nor to arrest
cancerous sand and mold, not even for
the dance of subway floods or the graceless
eclipse of all our promises and planets.

Home Ward

Seoul, Korea, 2012

Where was I to look?
Patients laid along both
long walls. There were
nurses scattered, weaving

through the patients, my
wheharabuhji's arms tied
to each side of his small
bed to prevent pulling of

tubes out of his long arm,
white gauze wrapped so
taut he could not lift his
hand. Walking down the

small halls created by the
elderly bodies, any bed
might have been his. My
eyes tossed well between

skinny plots, my breath
held to avoid their
contents, slow molding. I
had not had to search for

that face, the smile that
declares. His two detained
liabilities were so thin to
me, a stranger holding

his hand. Their theory:
our elders are less lonely
in these rooms of sweat
and whimpers. I dream of

him for the first time,
months later, silhouette
body filled again, strong
and smiling as we clutch.

In months he would be
dead in every way, but I
would not fly out, because
of my school schedule, the

cost of travel. Across the
northern border his other
descendants picture him
at thirty, father, frozen.

Sunset, Glory

There is a heavily chandeliered
gas station in California, and if
you wonder if the night manager
has any new obsessions lately,

one is positioning the tradeoff
between flexibility and strength
as a modern development, and
another is considering talk of

weather as a way of making
mood public in other places (like
we use traffic). Also, a dosed
expansion of the octave range.

And then a joke I won't share
now because it only works
if you agree the idea of god is
hilarious. Mine: care as control,

moth wrestling as pageantry,
the intricacy of wiring the moon
would require if we lit it
ourselves, and scheduling

space to mourn a migraine as
it ends—the calm—the ceiling far,
and jeweled, and bright, brighter

River

It's not true that sand is
uncountable. Everything
is when you have enough
time, vats. The woods,
inevitably, are satire
to the counter, who is
a keeper, not a consumer.
Carving motes, you can
get faster, more or yes
invisible. Just a rumor
that anything shatters,
no, one day you round
the brown trail and, oh, a
funeral—one afternoon you
open a bag of chips and
inside there's an orchid.

Mama I Am Sorry

For the stillbirth and the live ones. For
my books, degrees, and all the other

ways I have betrayed you. For unlinking
our arms a dozen times the year before

your surgery, unconvinced you needed
the relief until the afternoon I walked

up from the subway station—and that
before you saw me, I then watched you

on the street, alone without even a rail,
lurching and winding. The calls, of

course, that I did not return, the care I
would not acknowledge out of cowardice

and a hope to never need you or to need
anyone. For every question I refused

to answer, or did not answer generously.
For remembering the orange juice you

put in the guacamole and the sprouts
washed in hot water. That this list, like

your prescription deliveries and the group
chats, will end before either of us is ready.

About the rug you saved for, and the man
who pretended not to speak the street

language, your holding up the cash as you
pointed to what you wanted. *I'm sorry,*

he said, *I can't understand you.* You know,
umma, that I am sorry differently; I promise

you I will not say it to be cruel or polite:
that never will I be so banal, so American.

Faint

Vagueness tends to criminalize
and of few available alternatives
my favorite is the dream of the same

room. Pick your noise, in wells
or against walls. In the light

of the microwave clock, under advice
of long symbols, showily I become

my own guest (in mother words,
a duty). Oxygen a calm oddity
everywhere but its status more

bounced in bias. To be my chorus,
I first had to be a teenager who hoped

to kill the myth of the protagonist,
related quarries. Mental trespasses then

of floating down from tall towers
denoted the promise of language's
end. In its icon of bloodlessness,

my skin had, has, the potential
to be a good canvas for the palettes

of others. I'm not native to any
place and so naive to every log—

still want the trees less naked.

Setting

The aural chronicle of this town is written
in jukebox codes and corn miles, the wind

shifting with the harvest and in the bar back
entrance. Everyone here is young in a way,

proud of their coldness in another, and even
so, fixed into the deer bush with the shoes

we chose upon arrival. We were warned
and still we are convinced of our status

as inventors and as casualties. So many
of us left hometowns for this, bringing

our versions of shakshuka (mine florid,
too dense). Our language is an interim one

of copays, porch swings, and the deadening
issue, by which we hope not to eventually

relax into a lack of feeling, making of
mortality a chasm waned. So we pay

tips we cannot afford, and realize
veterinarians are contracted by owners

of animals, not animals. A place that takes
crawling, transcribing, while the music, fire

pit seem to run all night. People here choose
this every day, knowing in planned

suburbs and merciful cities, they gossip
less but read less also. We aim toward

the pleas of our childhood, to one day live
in a drawn house: big, crowded, ours for

the year. When we depart, it will be earlier
in the morning than we ever woke all the years

here and we will concede then that our self-
serving arguments, these illusions, were griefs.

Sheds

Harps can be rented
and vague like cities
hope to be and besides,

dignity is not my priority
right now. The book on how
light behaves bedside,

weeds sheerer
uncombed. Doled and
arranged evenly, they become

wed to the grave dances
and scrape snow, in chant
form. I hem the cove,

arrange the chalk, its
scrapped occasion, because
out in the blue, helmed

by cover and coast,
most come to an image
margined—the way we

choose our parents (that
is, eventually). Me, my
body makes a plan.

"How Is Temperature in East?"

We leaving tomorrow.
Call me to say bye I
lo---- ve you
              Be lazy
you deserve it. I am so
exiting thinking Santa
Babara trip. We had
gone you were four years
old.
     I didn't know I will
be this age and feel tired
so easy and keep
forget everything. You are
in your precious times.
But don't forget you
will be my age and regret
things. Don't try to do more
thing or care too many
people.
          How cold? I
hope you walk underground
path Sometimes cold wakes
us up. In korea I like winter
pretty much I like desire
for surviving more than any
season We were hungry
too. Good luck
          How is
your feeling? I will pray
every morning for you. Sorry
that I am not good mother
who you can share everything.
But trust me
         I love you more

than I had loved you.
                                    You
are so mature to understand
old analog emotion.
                            I want
to say sorry I didn't share
enough your pain when you
are that young. Thank you
for get over your special
difficulty. I love you and
strange to say I respect
you. This centrury is too
dry I am happy you have
emotion
                    Don't skip any
meal. If you miss, you
can't get meal forever. I
just tell you that you have
strong will to overcome
the situation.
                            Don't forget
you are million times
precious than money. I
hope you had a good day

north Korea So terrible.
We will send more corns
next month.
                        I have heard
your cousin cried on her 30th
B-day last week. You guys
didn't say to her. Bad
sisterhood. Send her
something. E card, etc.

Ceremony

I compose cakes mostly
and paint stationery when done
burying articles, sparing
pronouns. Awake, I need to be

draped the way noise can
be extracted from an image
at the far end of the strip
mall where, asleep, I wander

weekly. I crouch below the storm
window of the eastmost
closet, dodge death by hoses,
and one night on a green, I say:

no, it's not a pig, it's a goldfish.
A goldfish can't survive
on the ground, what is it—
Some nights I seek welding

help, walk on the freeway,
prefer summer curls, read origami,
keep jars inside fish and giant
asparagus in warm water. I hide

a book and the keys, carry someone
else's baby past the wedding
security. Mornings, speech is
edited, lamps have levers, and

my faucets are theory
as other lungs become

haunted. In a dream a former lover
and her new lover and their

old lover recite a poem
titled a summer date. My sister
recognizes it and I think,
all there is left now is—

Answering My Great-Grandmother

No action is told in a Buddhist poem,
        but I'm not a Buddhist and this is only

a part-time poem. I won't lie for a line,
        not even to say someone owes you

desire. The feeling of the South is the feeling
        of being in the middle of nowhere

and it being quiet—it's an alignment
        issue, and a crowding problem.

My foot stays broken, my finger still bent,
        but as you know I'm not a runner,

not a pianist. I like a socially reasonable
        amount of blood and discipline.

It's early, it's blue—let's take a fantasy
        of fusion and eat off the ground

while I keep faith in trains and other modes
        of tchotchke distribution.

Degeneration

A generation of children learned only the language of the raiders. Except when teachers of their kind, breaking oaths to the state, kept the original language on pamphlets taped to desk bottoms. After language, the raiders took land, and the raided paid rent in girls. The raiders then forced worship, and new names. Later they would tell us and everyone who would listen that it was they who brought industry, technology. They left now long ago, and the pamphletted alphabet became the only again. But that generation of children is aging—and as their brains loosen, with stroke or dementia or exhaustion, they inherit such dormant music, are carried into those policed classrooms. It could make anyone laugh—to think that when they cannot recognize their apartments, their bodies, or each other, they know that language, the language of the raiders which, in hiding, has become primary. Smiling at ceilings, they speak the words they did not teach their children.

Signs

There is an island claimed by two small countries, in a sea whose naming is also disputed by those countries. One recently occupied the other, which became dependent and furious, and many feelings of disgust and memories of penetration remain. Though it is referred to as an island when it is in the news, which is often in these two countries (a deed found in newly released government documents, or an even older map referencing it by its cover name), the island is a group of two rocks with ground, and many smaller rocks that do not fit humans. Seagulls fly between them in the summer, and their only two true residents take a boat. The fisherman and his wife come from the more recently wartorn country, where sea levels are rising fastest in the region. The fishing has no heirs, but the lighthouse officials plan to stay past the fisherman, who everyone hears has been going blind.

Home Ward

Koreatown, Los Angeles, 2021

Where was I to look? My chin-harabuhji gasped with his eyes closed in the far right corner of the humid room. He had been rejected from this nursing home for pulling out the stomach tube that had replaced all his food and drink. Eventually, when he was so weak he could not reach for it, he was admitted.

My nurse cousin and I raged at the regimen. He was grunting, brows so overlapping in furrow, fly left on his face. Morphine would dull his ability to cough up his phlegm, they said; his livelihood depended on his constant discomfort. But it was not hours, but weeks. He died alone,

discovered some hours later, as recorded.

Some of us touched his corpse, criticizing the mortician's rough handling of the body on the cart. Some watched from outside the window, kneeling. The only other patient in the room grunted behind his curtain, dissatisfied with the visitors received by the cadaver that day, an exception to the times that killed him.

In my dream a week later, he tells us how awful it had been when he could not have water.

Surrounded, as he would have been by heirs the night that stroke struck.

When the sponge grazed his lips during baths in bed, he would kiss the air, gaping for liquid. He rarely smiled in life, though softened by illness, my halmoni's and his. In the dream, he laughs, as though at the relief of a passed pain.

At the End

Think of the mushroom
soaked and near-dissolved,
of the shrouded smile at
the terminal or the fish

whose stripes appear only
on cooking through. Think
through the thrown tantrums
and basketballs, the berries

unpicked in a heat wave
or the yawn interrupting
itself. Think on the photo
unglossed at the crease, the orchid

outlasting the graveyard
visits, the leavings of
the resolute sticker and
even the invited weight

of an awning or a title.
To think about any being,
summon a kind of waist,
about the glassy dress

shoes on the connecting
flight, the veins memorized
in illness, the temporary
cover for the grand and sleepless

windows. Fold each thought, word
to word: the highway stop where
toilet paper is piled, the knife
marks on the counter with

the ants carrying earwax,
the wooden enclosure for
a lake, flooded, the hum of
the cobbled afterparty. Think.

Residue Guidelines

I was told not to shake
        my foot that way—
        the luck leaks out

your restless limbs—
        so could you sit
        more glassily

and not leave the pillows
        upright, another hollow
        place to ward away your

fortune. I feared young
        dying, hating to
        waste, but lately

when I cough or clot blood I
        register this potential as
        passed, my age

now emblem of having aged:
        nothing to be envious of,
        nothing to revere.

I survived past fulfilling
        other's schemas for decades
        and I offer you

the grammar of this chance:
        keep your hair
        unwashed to hold

its knowledge and
        avoid writing
        your name, or anyone's,

in red except the dead
        or those you wish
        to be dead soon.

Nights turn off your
        fans, collect
        your toenail

clippings, and refuse
        hums so you dream
        of persimmons and

pigs. And if you have loved
        then be early, even
        earlier, to the after

death ceremony and
        when you kiss
        the other grievers

as you listen to
        the chants, force your legs
        greenly still.

Notes

Poems from this volume first appeared in *The Baffler, Bennington Review, Black Warrior Review, The Brooklyn Rail, Colorado Review, Conjunctions, Denver Quarterly, Electric Literature, The Kenyon Review, The Madison Review, The Margins, The Massachusetts Review, Michigan Quarterly Review, Narrative, The Nation, New England Review, Poetry, Poetry Daily, Poetry London, Poetry Northwest, Poetry Society of America, Rhino, The Sewanee Review, Southern Humanities Review, Sugar House Review, Ugly Duckling Presse, Washington Square Review,* and *The Yale Review.* Many true thanks to their editors and staffs.

"Orientation": Nate, the friend addressed, gives his love to this poem's publication and its abolitionist hopes.

"'P.S. Please Forgive Poor Grammar'" and "'How Is Temperature in East?'": Emails my mother sent me between 2011 and 2013 have been ruptured and remade with her blessing.

"Before the DMZ": Over five months in 1983, the show <이산가족을 찾습니다> (*Finding Dispersed Families*) ran for more than 450 hours with over 50,000 people aired trying to reunite with family. The poem maps the divided Koreas with the current boundary, which in 1953 supplanted one by latitude.

"Pale Music": The mountain line is a motif of conversations with my friend Wazhma and her family.

"Composition of a Raft": "We" includes and thanks Zeina, Saffiyah, Andom, Zahiah, and Suba.

"Leave Her to Heaven": The title is taken from a 1945 movie.

"Ten Sessions": The text of my former short-term therapist's notes is used and transformed with her permission.

"In Atlanta": Memories shared by Sharonlyn, said matriarch, are of Montgomery in 1967; at a news conference one day after the 2021 shootings, a police spokesperson said of the shooter: "yesterday was a really bad day for him, and this is what he did."

"Home Ward": The poems are rough blueprints of two hospice wards. Thanks to Diana Khoi Nguyen, who was crucial to their digital translation.

"Residue Guidelines": These directions for fortune have been gathered and overheard untrackably from my grandparents, their parents and siblings, my parents, their siblings, and my cousins.

Many who are or have been in psychiatric systems or abusive circumstances are dead or dying, and I word toward a world in which outliving their structures is not dependent on timing, power, and luck.

Acknowledgments

Thank you to Rae Armantrout for encountering this book with grace and to everyone at Yale University Press who cared for it through publication.

I am grateful to the next readers of *Ward Toward*—Monica Youn, Donika Kelly, and Allison Adelle Hedge Coke—for reflecting back to me its conscious substance. Thank you, Etel Adnan, for offering a visual measure of my wards and words for the cover, and Simone Fattal for making it possible.

The manuscript was written with and encouraged by fellowships from MacDowell, Ucross Foundation, Hambidge Center, Vermont Studio Center, Poetry Foundation, and the Truman Capote Literary Trust. I appreciate these gifts of material support and gathering among artists, which was as sustaining.

Thank you to my partner, this collection's most essential and gracious editor and surest friend.

My thanks to the many teachers and students (past, present, and future) who make my life in writing not only possible but also playful, rigorous, and surprising.

Finally, and always, I am thankful to my friends and family, who are each to me what language can only approach being: whole and unmediated.